Walking in the Wolds
with Hugh Marrows

Acknowledgements

Like most authors I owe a debt to many helpers, in many capacities – not least to those who before me have written so eloquently about the various aspects of Lincolnshire's landscape, history and people, and whose work I have plundered in my research; I offer my thanks to all of them.

A big "Thank-you" must also go from me to the editors of the Lincolnshire Newspapers who have given me the opportunity to have my work published in their papers.

My thanks too must go to my wife (and part time secretary) who has accompanied me on some of these walks, and allowed me days out to reconnoitre others. I have not always been alone even then and I mention with gratitude my friend David Cross who has been with me on several of the rambles in this book – and many others too – and who has always uncomplainingly walked where I have asked him.

Others who deserve mention too include Jenny White who has helped me out with some digital photography, the staff at the Lincolnshire County Archaeology Service who have patiently dealt with many phone calls and letters over the years, and finally the landlords of those inns where we make use of their carparks.

Hugh Marrows

First Published in 2007 by:
Lincolnshire Newspapers Ltd
5-6 Church Lane, Boston, Lincolnshire,
PE21 6ND
in conjunction with
At Heart Ltd, 32 Stamford Street, Altrincham,
Cheshire, WA14 1EY.

Text and images: Hugh Marrows

©2007 Lincolnshire Newspapers Ltd

ISBN: 978-1-84547-144-6

Printed and bound by Bell & Bain Ltd., Glasgow

Introduction

My country walks articles for Lincolnshire Newspapers first appeared in March 1999 and have continued almost without a break since then. From the outset they were written with two aims. Firstly as an attempt to both interest and inform readers about Lincolnshire's history and its enormous visual heritage seen in its landscape, archaeological remains, churches, castles, canals, abandoned railways and assorted curiosities – to name but a few! The second aim was to encourage people out into the countryside so that, through the medium of country walks, they would go and see these things for themselves. In the process I hoped too that they would discover places that they might otherwise not have done – perhaps even places they had not known about before! The walks were all kept deliberately short too in anticipation that perhaps readers of more mature years or those unaccustomed to rambling might be tempted to "give them a go", and that families might get involved too. And there are also the health benefits from the exercise involved!

The Lincolnshire Newspapers has now kindly decided to publish in book form a selection of walks from these last eight years work. We have decided to concentrate on The Wolds, an area that has since April 1973 been officially designated as an Area of Outstanding Natural Beauty and whilst forming perhaps a tenth of Lincolnshire's land area does contain much of its finest scenery – though I hasten to add, it certainly does not have a monopoly!

And so to the walks! The choice of routes is all mine, so if your favourite, is missing then I am to blame! Their locations stretch between the far north of the county where we can look across the Humber into Yorkshire, right the way down to the point at which the Wolds dramatically fall

Introduction

away to the Fens, with the final hills having quite outstanding views across the Wash to Norfolk. And on Walk 19 we go pretty close to the highest point in the whole county too! All the route descriptions have been updated and revised where necessary, and are presented in a standard format. There are new maps too!

A few practicalities may be worth a mention. Walking is an inexpensive recreation and in spite of what rambling magazines might say, for outings such as these a lot of expensive equipment is not really necessary. Clothing is a common sense matter to suit the season and prevailing weather (and all these walks are easy half day ones!) but do get the best boots you can afford – waterproofing and comfort really are important here! And the same goes for waterproof jackets! Another worthwhile investment is maps. I always recommend the Ordnance Survey Explorer series; they are drawn to a larger scale and contain much more detail than the Landrangers. Whilst the route descriptions will get you round each walk without a map I still recommend that you take one. They not only allow you to interpret your wider surroundings and put each walk in context but will also enable you to locate start points and some points of interest more easily. I have used grid references quite frequently in both the text and the "About the Walk" sections too as location aids and on each OS map you will find an explanation and a working example of this simple but invaluable map reading technique. It's always worth knowing exactly where you are, in order to plan an alternative route in an emergency for example! Food is clearly a question of personal preference of course but most walks have an inn or café nearby and many have picnic spots recommended; though of course picnics are very much a personal thing too! Nevertheless carrying a small emergency supply of food and drink is a sensible precaution!

Almost all the routes use rights of way throughout, but there are a few exceptions and these are clearly mentioned and described. Many farmers now open up land under the DEFRA Countryside Stewardship Scheme but it is important to remember that these paths and "Access Areas" do not appear on OS maps. You will however find that any such area or permissive path will also have a detailed map on display at each access point.

This book will, I hope, provide ideas and inspiration to readers to get out to explore and enjoy what Lincolnshire has to offer. I hope too that there is something in it for all tastes and abilities.

One final thing – wherever you are please obey the Countryside Code! It makes life so much pleasanter for other ramblers following in your footsteps, and for the farmers and landowners on whose goodwill we all rely!

Happy rambling!
Hugh Marrows

20 Wolds Walks

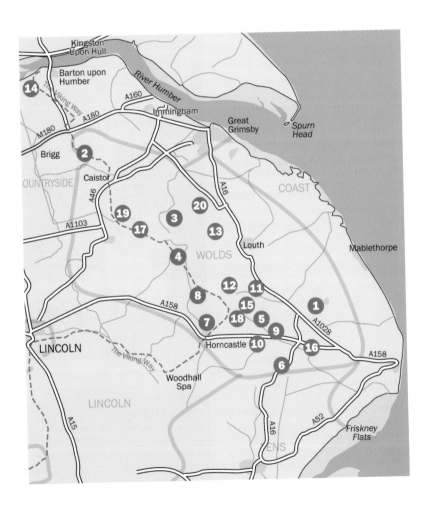

Walk 1 Alford Tothby & Rigsby
4 miles : 6.5 kilometres
OS Map: Landranger 122 (Skegness) : Explorer 274

Walk 2 Bigby and the Viking Way
6 miles : 9.6 kilometres
OS Map: Landranger 112 (Scunthorpe):Explorer 281

Walk 3 Binbrook
4 miles : 6.5 kilometres
OS Map: Landranger 113 (Grimsby):Explorer 282

Walk 4 Biscathorpe & East Wykeham
6 miles : 9.6 kilometres
OS Map: Landranger 122 (Skegness): Explorer 282

Walk 5 Brinkhill & Somersby
5 miles : 8 kilometres
OS Map: Landranger 122 (Skegness):Explorer 273

Walk 6 East Keal & Toynton All Saints
4 miles : 6.5 kilometres
OS Map: Landranger 122 (Skegness):Explorer 273

Walk 7 Far Thorpe & West Ashby (from Fulletby)
5 miles : 8 kilometres
OS Map: Landranger 122 (Skegness): Explorer 273

Walk 8 Goulceby & Red Hill
3 miles : 4.8 kilometres
OS Map: Landranger 122 (Skegness): Explorer 273

Walk 9 Hagworthingham & Bag Enderby
4 miles : 6.5 kilometres
OS Map: Landranger 122 (Skegness): Explorer 273

Walk 10 Hagworthingham, Snipe Dales & Winceby
5 miles : 8 kilometres
OS Map: Landranger 122 (Skegness): Explorer 273

Walk 11 Ruckland, The Bluestone Heath Road & Farforth
5 miles : 8 kilometres
OS Map: Landranger 122 (Skegness): Explorer 273

Walk 12 Scamblesby Circuit
6 miles : 9.6 kilometres
OS Map: Landranger 122 (Skegness):Explorer 273

Walk 13 South Elkington & Acthorpe
Walk A – 3 miles : 4.8 kilometres
Walk B – 3 miles : 4.8 kilometres
OS Map: Landranger 122 (Skegness): Explorer 273

Walk 14 South Ferriby & Horkstow
5 miles : 8 kilometres
OS Map: Landranger 112 (Scunthorpe): Explorer 281

Walk 15 South Ormsby, Brinkhill & Driby
5 miles : 8 kilometres
OS Map: Landranger 122 (Skegness): Explorer 273

Walk 16 Spilsby & Halton Holegate
4 miles : 6.5 kilometres
OS Map: Landranger 122 (Skegness): Explorer 274

Walk 17 Tealby & Walesby
4 miles : 6.5 kilometres
OS Map: Landranger 113 (Grimsby): Explorer 282

Walk 18 Tetford & Salmonby
4 miles : 6.5 kilometres
OS Map: Landranger 122 (Skegness): Explorer 273

Walk 19 Walesby & Normanby-le-Wold
4 miles – 6.5 kilometres
OS Map: Landranger 113(Grimsby): Explorer 282

Walk 20 Wold Newton & Beesby
4 miles – 6.5 kilometres
OS Map: Landranger 113 (Grimsby): Explorer 282

Alford Tothby & Rigsby

This route from Alford includes a modest climb to the nearby Wolds hilltop hamlet of Rigsby that gives extensive views over the marsh to the sea.

Alford was mentioned in the Domesday Book and has had a market charter since 1283. It developed around the "ford by the alder trees", which ran through the stream (now bridged) beside the Manor House in West Street. This beautiful building, standing on the site of an earlier Elizabethan house, dates from 1661 and is now the Tourist Office. The other two most striking buildings in the town are the church and the windmill. Much of St. Wilfred's dates from the 14th century though considerable restoration took place in 1869. There is plenty of fine carving inside, but note especially the two-storied porch, once a school. It is believed that Captain John Smith from nearby Willoughby, the soldier, adventurer and governor of Virginia whose life was saved by the Indian princess Pocahontas, received some of his education here. The windmill has five sails and dates from 1837.

Now fully restored it is open to the public and has a tearoom. (Tel. 01507/462136 for times.)

In 1630 Alford was infected by the plague and (like Eyam in Derbyshire) voluntarily cut itself off from all outside contact. Food and supplies were placed outside the town and payment left in hollowed stones filled with vinegar to disinfect it. One of these was at Miles Cross on the A1104 close to Rigsby.

The lands of Rigsby parish were given by William the Conqueror to his half brother Bishop Odo of Bayeau but it never seems to have been a large village, for the population in 1862 was only 96, and was down to 16 by 2000. The church is dedicated to St. James and may, being of Saxon origin, have been one of the first in the area. The present building dates from 1863

and was designed by James Fowler of Louth, in what was then the popular Neo-Gothic style. The cost was £865 and apparently all the labourers in the parishes of Rigsby and Ailby gave a week's wages towards this sum. Fowler's church replaced one of chalk with a thatched roof, (there is a picture of it inside) though he retained some remnants of Norman masonry. Also on display is a (probably) 15th century sword and helmet found in the churchyard in 1872 and an octagonal 14th century font.

Walk 1

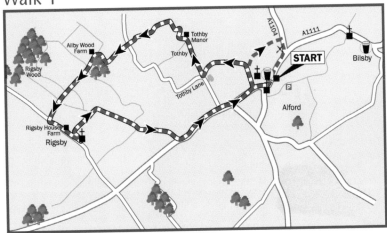

START : Millers Way carpark (near church), Alford. [GR466761]

OS MAPS : Landranger 122 (Skegness) : Explorer 274.

DISTANCE : 4 miles : 6.5 kilometres.

REFRESHMENTS : Inns and cafés and tearooms in Alford.

From the carpark cross the road and turn left through the churchyard onto High Street. Continue to the Manor House in West Street, and there turn right along Park Lane to a gate at the end. (The footpath to the right leads to the windmill if you choose to come back this way.) Our walk however bears half left to another gate in a hedge. Cross a second meadow to its far corner, ignore a footpath going right, and maintain your direction onto a grass track. When this joins a farm road turn right.

At a two way footpath sign, just before Tothby Manor go over the adjacent stile aiming to the left of the house where the field narrows. From a further stile near a drinking trough walk to the right of a tin shed to another stile by a gate. Turn left alongside a dyke and at its corner, where there is a waymark, go right for 100 yards over an arable field to the next waymark by a hedge corner. Now turn left beside the hedge until you reach a footbridge on your right. Cross this, turning left along the field edge to soon zigzag over a ditch at waymarks. Continue to a road.

Follow the lane opposite and bear right at some woods where the lane now becomes a track that climbs gradually to the road near Rigsby. (Look back occasionally to admire the far reaching views.) Go left until you reach the green gate and footpath sign at Rigsby church.

Through the gate a grassy track swings left towards Rigsby House. In a few yards

look for a stile in the fence to your right and from it walk downhill, going slightly left in the direction of the woods alongside the next meadow. From a stile at the bottom proceed beside the woods to a 4-way footpath sign. Now turn sharp right to a stile and footbridge in the far hedge and go along a field edge path to a seat in the corner. After a rest turn right a few yards, then left at a footbridge, through a hedge gap, and along another field edge for 200 yards. Cross another bridge and then turn immediately right beside a hedge to a further footbridge. Keep forward to a kissing gate at the A1104 road, opposite Toll Bar Cottage.

Turn left and walk back into Alford. To visit the windmill, either return along Park Lane from the Manor House (and then turn right) or continue from the carpark along East Street. ■

Bigby And The Viking Way

This route visits an area with outstanding views plus a delightful section of the Viking Way.

We begin at Bigby. Limited parking is possible near the phone box at the bottom of Bigby Hill; otherwise park with consideration in the village. Refreshments are only available off route in Grasby. Note that a short distance near Grange Farm, Somerby is rough underfoot and that two shorter routes of 4 or 5 miles are explained in the route instructions. OS Explorer map 281 is double-sided; use both sides to cover the full walk.

The western slopes of the Wolds presented ideal settlement sites to the Danish invaders arriving during the eighth century. Their popularity is evident from the many villages with the Old Danish "by" endings. This walk alone passes four: Owmby, Searby, Somerby and Bigby. These sites offered low-lying wetlands (the Ancholme valley was then of course undrained), a spring line on the hillsides, meadow, woodland and higher ground suitable for ploughing.

The first village on our route is Bigby, "Bekki's" farmstead. All Saints' church here is worth visiting for it has several unusual features including a rood beam carved in 1929 in Oberammergau. The "pièce de resistance" however is the tomb to Sir Robert Tyrwhitt and his wife Bridget (a maid to Queen Elizabeth I) surrounded by carvings of their 22 children. The village has no WWII memorial, for quite remarkably all ten men who went to war from Bigby returned.

Above the village Bigby Top gives outstanding views over the Wolds, towards Humberside airport and to Wrawby post mill, the only one left in Lincolnshire. A little further on we walk beside Hendale Woods, part of the 1848 "great plantings" when the Earl Yarborough planted 12 million trees on his estate. Pelham's Pillar (near Caistor) commemorates the achievement.

Searby provides additional confirm-ation of the Danish link for its name means the "Seafarers" homestead. The church here (St. Nicholas) was built in 1832 in what architects call white brick, though to you and I it looks yellow. Inside is a west gallery and the screen, together with the pulpit, organ case and benches, were carved by the Rev. Townsend, vicar here for 44 years in the l9th century. This DIY vicar also turned his hand to bricklaying and in 1866 built the inscribed "Rest and Be Thankful" shelter opposite the church gate.

At Somerby the little church of St. Margaret's squats on a hillside ledge. The tower is 700 years old but the rest was restored in 1844, no doubt explaining the carving against the door, apparently depicting Queen Victoria. Nearby in the hall lived Sir Edward Weston who became Secretary for Ireland. In an adjacent field our walk passes the enormous monument erected by him in thanks for his happy life at Somerby and 29 years of marriage.

Walk 2

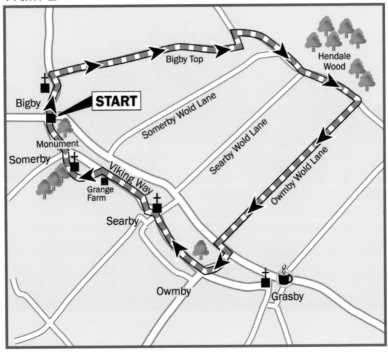

START : Bigby village. [GR059072]

OS MAPS : Landranger 112 (Scunthorpe) : Explorer 281.

DISTANCE : 6 miles : 11.6 kilometres.

REFRESHMENTS : Cross Keys, Grasby (Off route : 1 mile return) [GR089050]

Set off through Bigby village. Some 200 yards beyond the church look for a footpath climbing the slope to your right, which soon levels out to join a track past Bigby Top barn. In just over a mile bear left at a 3-way footpath sign to meet a green lane. Here bear sharply back to the right and continue until you are beside Hendale Wood. (Along this section you will pass two paths going right, both easily navigated, which head down to Somerby and Searby respectively. These two alternatives both rejoin the main walk.)

Walk alongside the woods for 200 yards before turning right down Owmby Wold Lane to reach the A1084 road (approx. a mile and a half). Cross over and turn left, and then right down towards Owmby. Before reaching the village a footpath (the Viking Way) crosses the road by a seat. (Here a left turn onto a good path takes you into Grasby for the Cross Keys inn.)

Otherwise turn right. A delightful path, easily followed, now leads through woods and meadows directly into Searby. Go into Back Lane, to the left of the church, following it round to the left and then crossing the footbridge on your right. Pass a pond, veering slightly right to the field corner. In the next field walk up a rough headland with a hedge on your right and from the

stile at the top keep forward past the farmhouse to another stile at the farm road. Follow this to reach the public road.

Walk ahead until you can descend leftwards into Somerby churchyard, where behind the tower a path leads to a lane. Bear right, and right at a road, then in a few yards turn left into the field containing the Weston monument. Beyond that go slightly downhill to a stile then cross one more field back into Bigby. ■

Binbrook

Typical Wolds countryside surrounds Binbrook, through which the outward section of this walk switches back along quiet roads, whilst the return contours along high ground with magnificent views over the hillsides and the village.

Underfoot this walk is good throughout, so progress can be rapid! The anti-clockwise direction gets the most strenuous part over first and covers the road part early on too, which I always like to do if possible. It also ensures that the best views are on the return leg too. Park in Binbrook Market Place; but readers doing the walk who would like to patronise the inn may park at The Plough instead. This is Binbrook's only pub and alterations and additions to it over the years mask its true age, and at first sight you might not now guess at its mid 1700s origins.

"Binnibroc" was here at Domesday and was granted a market in 1633, the wide Market Place standing testament to its former importance.

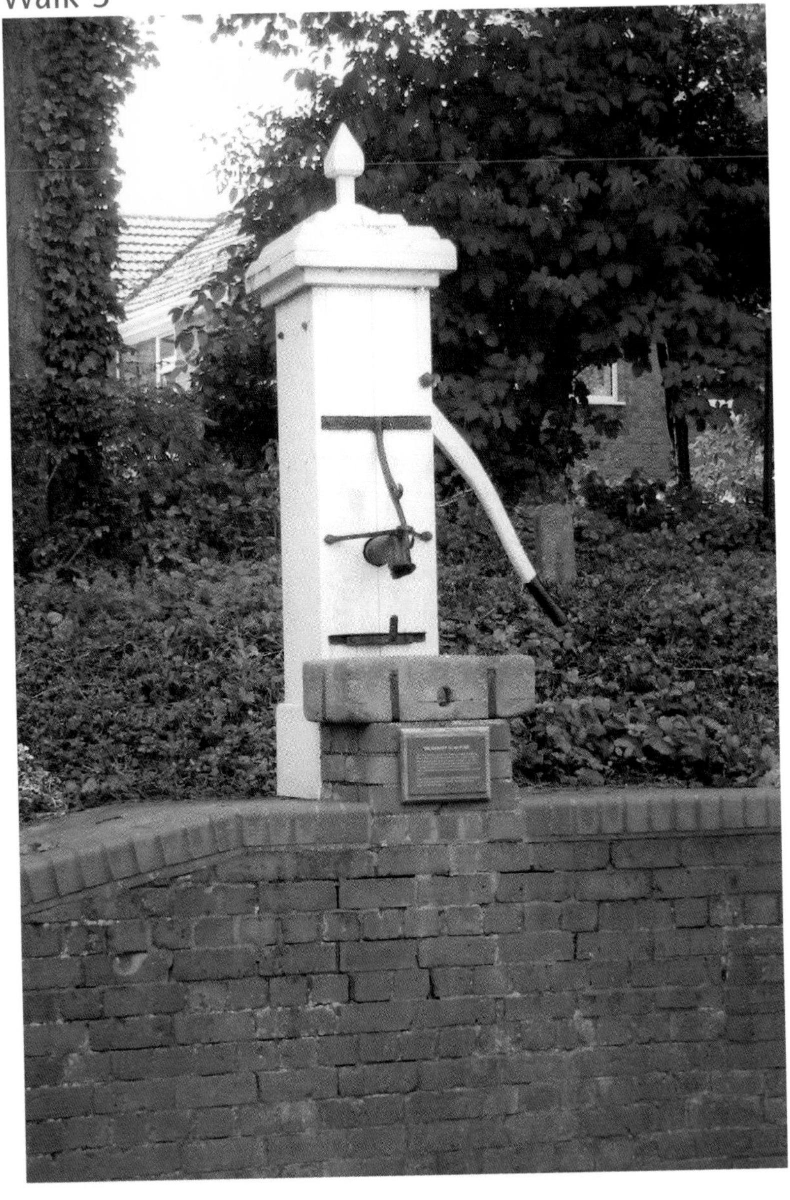

The village pump still stands here, opposite the Manor House, an elegant 18th century building with some beautiful and unusual windows. This small market town was once divided into two parishes, St. Gabriel's and St. Mary's, each with its own church. Derelict by 1822, St. Gabriel's site is now a small park near to where Grimsby Road enters the Market Place. St. Mary's was demolished in 1867 and the "new" church, designed by James Fowler the famous Louth architect, erected in 1869. As a consequence this explains its dedication to both Saints.

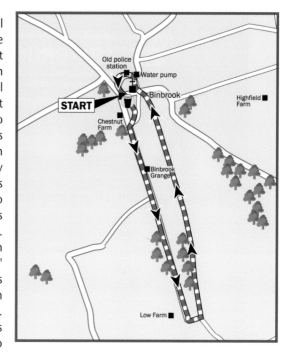

Also in Grimsby Road, and now a private residence, is the Old Police Station built in 1852, which contained cells and a magistrate's room. Opposite is another water pump built to supply local hill farmers for, amongst other uses, their own brewing at harvest time. It is designed so that water carts could be filled and the old horse tethering rings are still let into the wall. All these features are seen towards the end of the walk.

ABOUT THE WALK

START : Market Place, Binbrook [GR210939]

OS MAPS : Landranger 113 (Grimsby) : Explorer 282.

DISTANCE : 4 miles : 6.5 kilometres.

REFRESHMENTS : Plough Inn, Binbrook.

From the Market Place leave past the Plough Inn or exit the inn's carpark and turn right. Pass the

Old Rectory and turn left down Spring Hill. At the bottom turn right along St. Mary's Lane ignoring the footpath sign opposite the end of South Rise. At the lane end keep forward on a grass path below Low House and by the edge of a large garden until you reach a stile. Cross this and bear right past another garden to a second stile onto Ludford Road.

Turn left to leave Binbrook and at a junction, in just over half a mile, keep forward along a narrow side road for another mile. All this time you will be travelling in a straight line (on the map) but with several steep rises and dips, but in quiet and peaceful scenery surrounded by woods and fields. The road eventually bears sharp left.

In another 150 yards, when it bends to the right, look for the footpath sign pointing leftwards. Go through the hedge and cross a field heading for the right hand corner of the woods on the far side. Walk alongside these, and then go slightly left over a farm track, before continuing with more woods on your right. Now simply keep ahead, passing behind a small copse at one stage, until the path drops steeply down to the edge of Binbrook village. There are wonderful views all the way along this hillside.

After descending to the road turn left to reach a footpath on the right below the churchyard. Visit the church first if you wish, then follow this footpath through to Grimsby Road turning left to pass the old Police Station and the farmer's water pump. The former site of St. Gabriel's is to the right near the top just before you bear left again into the Market Place. ∎

Biscathorpe & East Wykeham

Lincolnshire has an abundance of deserted medieval villages and this walk visits one of the most interesting, high on the central Wolds.

The walk starts and finishes along part of the Viking Way and we begin from the church at Biscathorpe, which lies tucked away in a pretty valley a couple of miles north of Donington-on-Bain. There are no refreshments en route, though East Wykeham is suitable for a picnic. The nearest inn is the Black Horse in Donington-on-Bain only five minutes' drive from the start. [NOTE. A short section follows the A157; there is a pavement but watch children and pets carefully.]

Archaeologists refer to deserted medieval villages as DMV's and over 220 are known in Lincolnshire so our county has long been in the forefront of investigations into this particular aspect of medieval history. Although it had been known for centuries that many villages had disappeared, the advent of aerial photography proved a revelation as to the true extent of their numbers. (Incidentally Gainsthorpe in Lincolnshire was the first DMV ever to be photographed from the air in April 1925.) Many are on private land, but East Wykeham is open to all under the Countryside Stewardship Scheme. There you will see clearly visible streets, house platforms and even (most unusually) the remains of a church. East Wykeham is therefore the principal destination of this walk, although we see two other lost village sites en route.

We leave Biscathorpe to head for Burgh-on-Bain (pronounced "Bruff"!), a hilltop village of charming cottages with St. Helen's church presiding proudly over the main road. Some of the tower is Norman and there is Early English work inside too, but most dates from a Victorian (1874) restoration. A little further on at

Girsby we pass the magnificent gateway entrance to Girsby Manor, its pillars surmounted by stone foxes as a reminder of the name of the Fox family who once lived here. The 1840s house was demolished years ago and there is only a bungalow there now.

Nearby is West Wykeham, a fine DMV site, but unfortunately with no right of way to it. Nevertheless it is seen from our walk, its streets and house platforms clearly visible across the valley from our viewpoint half a mile away. (See the walk instructions below.)

East Wykeham however can be explored freely and you may stroll along its sunken streets or stand where cottagers once had their homes. A sizeable village was mentioned in the Domesday Book but later records show only one family remaining by 1563, and forty years later the church too was a ruin. Today's church remains, though picturesque, may perhaps have been partly devised as a folly visible from the nearby Hall.

Beside the Viking Way as we head back towards Biscathorpe lurks Grim's Mound (GR233870), a prehistoric burial site. On the hilltop in front of you looms Belmont TV tower; a fascinating contrast in technologies over the millennia.

ABOUT THE WALK

START : Biscathorpe church. [GR230849]

OS MAPS : 122 (Skegness) : Explorer 282.

DISTANCE : 6 miles : 9.6 kilometres.

REFRESHMENTS : Black Horse, Donington-on-Bain.

Head uphill from the footbridge that is just across the road from Biscathorpe church, aiming for a stile by some woods. Beyond these cross a lane and (leaving the Viking Way) climb a second stile to cross a meadow to a third, from which a path slants gradually leftwards downhill to Burgh-on-Bain mill. From there a track leads up to the village, joining the A157 opposite the church.

Turn left along the road for a quarter of a mile before crossing into the lane for Girsby. This quiet by-way passes the site of Girsby Manor to meet a

lane on the right heading for Girsby Top. This is Wykeham Lane where we rejoin the Viking Way. When you are near the barns of Girsby Top Farm look leftwards for the view over to the earthworks of West Wykeham. Beyond the farm the lane becomes a downhill track, which crosses the River Bain (a mere stream here) before heading uphill to arrive at East Wykeham.

Just beyond a cottage a large open area contains the site of East Wykeham village. Ahead is another cottage and our walk continues from there. First however turn left towards Wykeham Hall. The ruins of the church can be reached through a handgate on the right just before the Hall entrance; explore the remainder of the village site as you return.

From the second cottage a wide grass path leads to a three-way footpath sign. Turn right here. Back at the A157 cross into the lane opposite and in a little over half a mile rejoin your outward route. As you retrace your final steps to Biscathorpe you will (again) be crossing faint earthworks of another lost village here too. ■

Brinkhill & Somersby

The Wolds around Somersby is the countryside in which the poet Tennyson was born and grew up. We walk to Warden Hill, a great local viewpoint.

We begin from where wide verges allow parking. The route includes some steep hills.

The highest part of Warden Hill is suitable for a picnic. Otherwise there are inns nearby in Tetford (White Hart), South Ormsby (Massingberd Arms) or Hagworthingham (George and Dragon); plus cafés in Hagworthingham and at Stockwith Mill, near Harrington.

Lincolnshire's famous poet, Alfred Tennyson, was born at Somersby on the 6th August 1809. His father, George, had been rector there, and for Bag Enderby, since the previous year. He had entered the church after having been "passed over" in favour of the younger brother, Charles, for succession to the family fortunes. Charles went on to build Bayons Manor at Tealby.

Alfred, the fourth of George's twelve children, went to school at Louth and then on to Cambridge, returning to Somerby in 1831 on account of his father's ill health. He had written poetry since childhood and his first work, in conjunction with his brother Frederick, was published when he was 18 by Jacksons of Louth in 1827. (Their shop still stands in the Market Place) After finally leaving Lincolnshire in 1837 he quickly established himself as a major poet, becoming Poet Laureate in 1850 and marrying Emily Sellwood of Horncastle the same year. He died on the 6th October 1892 and is buried in Westminster Abbey. Somersby House, the Tennyson rectory, is still opposite the church but is a private residence and not open to the public.

St. Margaret's church still has the font in which Tennyson was baptised and contains a small exhibition about

his life and associations with both Somersby and Lincolnshire. Outside there is an original churchyard cross, a real rarity for most were destroyed during the Civil War, and above the porch a sundial dated 1751.

Nearby, and looking more like a castle, stands Somersby Grange, built in 1722, which is possibly a design of Sir John Vanbrugh, designer of Grimsthorpe Castle and of Castle Howard. A quarter of a mile away along the lane leading west to Salmonby is the stream immortalised in Tennyson's poem "The Brook".

Bag Enderby's church, built in 1407, is also dedicated to St. Margaret. Here the Roundheads destroyed the churchyard cross after the Battle of Winceby in 1643, so only a stump remains. Look for part of an ancient Saxon shield nailed to the porch door. Inside, some of the ancient glass came, inexplicably, from Crowland Abbey.

On a botanical note you will see Common Horsetail plants by the Warden Hill path and even more abundantly at Fox Covert. [GR352735] Resembling large green bottlebrushes, they are members of the Equisetaceae family, and a very ancient species, virtually identical to commonly found fossils in coal measure rocks (Carboniferous period) from 370 million years ago.

Walk 5

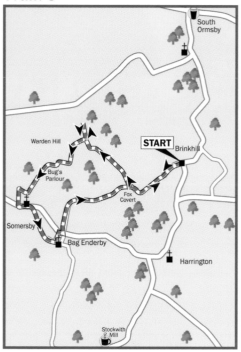

begin to climb the slopes of Warden Hill. In half a mile (and towards the top) make sure to look for a path that goes off to the left. Before following it however continue to the top (and even a short way down the other side) to savour the magnificent views.

Come back down – now turning right! When the path meets a farm road turn left, downhill past Fox Covert. Go steeply up again and bear right keeping to the track through a farm and descending past the oddly named "Bugs Parlour" woods to the road at Somersby.

Turn right for 100 yards and at the bend go left along a path beside a hedge to the next road. Turn left past Somersby House to the church.

After exploring continue along the road, keeping ahead at the "T" junction by the church and in a few yards turn right into White House farmyard. After the gate beyond the

ABOUT THE WALK

START : Green Lane, west of Brinkhill village. [GR369734]

OS MAPS : Landranger 122 (Skegness) : Explorer 273.

DISTANCE : 5 miles : 8 kilometres.

REFRESHMENTS : None on route.

Set off along Green Lane away from the road. The track soon bends right, then left, after which you should turn off to the right at a signposted path by a stream and

house turn left to a stile and go down the meadow to a double stile by a telegraph pole. From this proceed up to the top right hand field corner to another stile. Take a few paces forward and veer right, keeping to the next field edge as it curves round to the left. After a house join the lane up to Bag Enderby church.

Take the lane on the left before the church and at a "T" junction note the large hollow tree on the grass triangle (fun for children) before turning right. At the next junction go left into a track. Follow this for about a mile, rejoin the outward route and return to the start. ■

East Keal & Toynton All Saints

Before ending dramatically at East Keal, the Wolds conceals several little hidden valleys and our walk takes a leisurely stroll to explore some of them.

This route climbs the hills for their spectacular views, which in clear weather can extend across the Wash to Norfolk and Hunstanton. Mardon Hill is a highlight in this respect. Note to that the descent of Mardon Hill crosses two arable fields.

St. Helen's churchyard at East Keal provides our first viewpoint. Much of the church is 13th century and 14th century but the tower dates only from 1853. The south porch has some old carvings and (if you can get inside) the carvings on the font include, as an old church guide gleefully declares, a "bare backside"! There are more good views just beyond the nearby Old Rectory and between here and Toynton.

Toynton All Saints has a delightful little church that is something of a curiosity. Built of brick laid in English Bond (with alternate courses at right angles to each other) it appears all Georgian outside, but this brickwork is deceptive for inside gaps left in the plasterwork during the 1904 restoration reveal original medieval masonry. Beyond the church is another fine viewpoint.

Just up the road the village windmill stands on the site of a former post mill. The present one, built in the early 19th century, worked until the 1930s and in 1978 the internal gear was removed and re-fitted at Lincoln Mill where it remains today.

Later on the walk passes the Keal Carr nature reserve of the Lincolnshire Wildlife Trust. The woods here are mainly alder and because the stream has cut through the Spilsby Sandstone to underlying clay, bog and water plants flourish. Just beyond Glebe Farm we cross the far end of the reserve. The farm name serves as a reminder that it

was once owned by the local rector to provide extra income.

The climax of the walk is Mardon Hill. With a height of 288 feet (92 metres) it provides our final and best viewpoint with magnificent panoramas unfolding in all directions. Not surprisingly it was an air defence lookout point during WWII and has on OS trigonometric pillar at the summit.

ABOUT THE WALK

START : Lay-by near East Keal PO/shop. [GR380640]

OS MAPS : Landranger 122 (Skegness) : Explorer 273.

DISTANCE : 4 miles : 6.5 kilometres.

REFRESHMENTS : Shop at East Keal plus inns and cafés in nearby Spilsby

After parking at East Keal as suggested, follow Church Lane to its end beyond the churchyard at a stile and gate below the Old Rectory. Keep forward to another stile and from there bear left towards two gates. Climb the stile by the left hand one and descend to the Old Watermill in the valley. Cross the two footbridges onto an uphill track leading to a cattle grid and walk along Watermill Lane to reach Toynton church.

Enter the churchyard and pass round the church towards a hedge at the churchyard's far end, then turn right.

In the corner you will find a hedge gap and beyond it a footpath; turn left along it. At the second waymark, near an electricity pole, swing half left over rough ground (viewpoint!) down to a path junction near a fence. Go left and at a lane go left again. Once back in the village turn right.

Some 150 yards beyond the windmill cross the road into a new housing development and almost immediately turn right. Within a few yards a waymark on the left marks a path between a hedge and a fence, running parallel to the nearby drive. Carefully cross the A16 at Toynton Lodge and follow the grass track from the rear of the drive to a hollow with a 4-way footpath sign. Turn left on a track having the Keal Carr nature reserve away to your left.

On reaching Glebe Farm take the footpath on the left immediately after the house. Cross a shallow valley, climbing to a stile in a hedge corner and keep ahead to reach a road. Turn

right and in a quarter of a mile turn left at a "T" junction.

At the hilltop (opposite the Bolingbroke turn) take the signed path on your left through an unusual fieldgate and go through a second, small, wooden gate, inside and immediately on your right. From this go half left across the grassy field over the highest part of Mardon Hill. From a stile on the skyline maintain the same direction to a fingerpost in the next hedge near a telegraph pole then descend another field to a line of trees. Climb the stile in the fence ahead and walk to another one at a gate near farm offices. Now turn right along a gravel drive and when this bends left keep ahead to a white handgate by the A16. Turn left back to the start. ■

Far Thorpe & West Ashby (from Fulletby)

This walk, partly on the Viking Way, gives splendid views, and assuming clear weather has both Boston Stump and Lincoln Cathedral visible.

This walk is entirely on grass (paths or meadows), country lanes or farm tracks and my deliberately planned starting point at Fulletby Top means that the inn at West Ashby is passed near the halfway mark. The roadside has wide verges allowing ample parking space.

Fulletby is one of Lincolnshire's highest villages. Both Neolithic and Romano-British settlements are known in the vicinity whilst in the 1840s near Brook Farm (passed between Fulletby and Far Thorpe) Roman urns, bones and coins were found. This may seem less surprising when we remember that a Roman highway from Lincoln to Wainfleet and the Wash passed through nearby Ranby, Belchford and Tetford and villa farms close to such routes were quite common. The straight road followed during the early part of the walk is not Roman but was created in the 1770s when the surrounding land became subject to the Enclosure Acts. The wide protected verges are ablaze with wild flowers.

Before joining the River Bain the West Ashby Beck flows through a shallow valley once occupied by two villages. Although there are no visible remains now at Far Thorpe, the fields of present day Mid Thorpe overlie the lost village of Norcotes, and en route to West Ashby you will cross some of its remaining earthworks. The desertion and disappearance of many medieval villages (over 220 in Lincolnshire) often resulted from replacing arable farms with sheep pastures, and the consequent need for fewer labourers; though the Black Death in 1348/49 was in many cases a major factor too.

West Ashby village itself lies somewhat closer to the Bain valley and after the 1066 Norman invasion the land here was granted by William the Conqueror to his nephew Gilbert de Ghent. All Saints' church is built of greenstone, being mainly 15th century but much renovated in the 19th century. Inside on the chancel north wall a memorial describes in gruesome detail the death of Richard Calthrop, a local lad and naval midshipman on the Leander at the Battle of Algiers in August 1816. Nearby stands the beautiful Queen Anne style West Ashby House, with an imposing front doorway reputedly obtained in the 1930s from Captain Cook's London home.

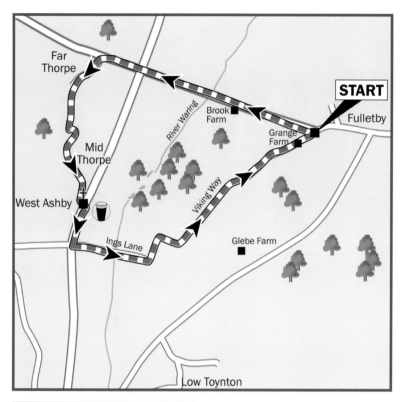

ABOUT THE WALK

START : West of Fulletby village. [Around GR291733]

OS MAPS : Landranger 122 (Skegness) : Explorer 273.

DISTANCE : 5 miles : 8 kilometres.

REFRESHMENTS : Green Dragon, West Ashby.

Locate the entrance to Grange Farm and from it follow the public road downhill past Brook Farm and over the River Waring rippling on its way to Horncastle. Beyond the river climb again to cross the A153 and then continue ahead into the secluded hamlet of Far Thorpe.

At a bridleway sign bear left into a lane and in 250 yards take the footpath bearing right by trees. Beyond an old millpond join a field headland path. Keep forward on this lovely grass path

by the beck, eventually bearing left by a large (and perhaps welcome) log seat to reach a footpath sign by a bridge and fieldgate. From this veer slightly right across a meadow to a stile in the high fence bordering a cottage drive. Turn left down the drive and then right at the road.

In a few yards go through the kissing gate on your left, before doubling back diagonally over a large meadow and crossing the faint medieval earthworks of Norcotes village as you do so. From another kissing gate by a telegraph pole maintain the same direction in a second meadow to a pair of kissing gates near the end of a brick wall. Keep right heading towards West Ashby church. Cross the stile on your right, just beyond a cottage, join

a lane, turn left and left again almost immediately into the churchyard. The Green Dragon is opposite.

Turn right (using the pavement!) along the A153 through the village until you can turn left into Ings Lane. Once across the River Waring again head uphill to make another left turn onto the Viking Way. (Look for the "Helmet" waymark.) Clearly marked, the path follows field edges as it heads steadily uphill back towards Fulletby. In half a mile the path cuts through a hedge. (It's just beyond here you may be able to see both Boston and Lincoln). Follow the far side of the hedge for a short way then bear right and complete the climb on a track through Grange Farm back to the start. ■

Goulceby & Red Hill

From the lovely village of Goulceby we explore part of the southern Wolds. The walk leads to the summit of Red Hill, a wonderful viewpoint.

(Note that the OS Explorer 273 omits a small section below Red Hill itself.) This is on Explorer 282, but this simple route is easily followed from the instructions without the extra map. The route is short and even with the climb to Red Hill (mostly gentle, but with a short steep bit near the top) is suitable for all ages.

Early in the walk we pass the little church of St. Peter at Asterby. Parts of it are 13th century but it has been much restored and added too over the centuries. It has been redundant since 1982.

Goulceby originated as a Danish settlement and was recorded as "Colchesbi" in the Domesday Book, with the "G" of its modern name appearing towards the end of the 13th century. when it had become known as "Golckesbi". Goulceby also lies on the Viking Way, which here follows the valley and its streams instead of the hilltops. Some of these streams and a picturesque ford are passed on the walk.

Over the centuries the village has shifted downhill from the high ground around its old churchyard, which we also visit. The present church however contrives to be both old and new at the same time, for its masonry was removed from the now isolated churchyard in 1908 and rebuilt at its present site, though even now it remains on the fringe of the village. Following the move and its consecration in 1909 All Saints suffered a rather embarrassing episode. In 1924 came the discovery that it had never been re-licensed for marriages and a special Act of Parliament was hastily passed to regularise the previous 15 years' wedding ceremonies.

Overlooking all this is Red Hill, a nature reserve managed by the Lincolnshire Trust. The geology here is interesting for it is one of only a few sites where you can see red chalk, a rock discoloured with iron as it was laid down in the warm, tropical seas of the Cretaceous Period some 135 to 160 million years ago. (Other outcrops are near Nettleton and in the cliffs at Hunstanton.) Red Hill's chalky soil supports many special plants, including vetches and orchids. There is an information board about the reserve, which is one of the Wolds finest viewpoints too, with a panorama extending as far as Lincoln Cathedral and makes it an ideal place for a picnic. On Good Fridays it is also the scene of a special Easter procession and service when three large crucifixes are set up on the hilltop.

By kind permission of the landlady readers may park and start from the Three Horseshoes inn at Goulceby, a great place for refreshment before or after your walk.

ABOUT THE WALK

START : Three Horseshoes, Goulceby. [GR254791]

OS MAPS : Landranger 122 (Skegness) : Explorer 273.

DISTANCE : 3 miles : 4.8 kilometres.

REFRESHMENTS : Three Horseshoes, Goulceby.

 From the inn car park turn right, keeping forward along Ford Way. In about 300 yards bear left down to the ford and cross by the footbridge – unless you fancy a paddle. In a few yards climb the stile on your right (with Viking Way waymarks), cross a meadow to another stile and then bear right over a boardwalk at a marshy area. Next cross a track and continue by a stream. At the next stile turn left by a hedge and at the field top go half right over a rise and an arable field and gain the road near Asterby church.

Walk 8

There turn left and walk to the next junction. Opposite this a footpath begins on your right. Level at first it then rises gradually with a final short, steep section through trees to the top of Red Hill. This wonderful viewpoint is a great place for a picnic and the nature reserve, deserves exploration. (The red chalk cliff itself however is steep, loose and dangerous!)

Continue by following the road downhill and at the bottom cross into Manor Farm. Go through the farmyard, then along a clear path with stiles for half a mile (ignore paths going to left or right) into Goulceby's old churchyard. In the lane beyond we join the Viking Way and turn left. At a road take the path opposite; but first go left a short way to visit the church. When the path ends climb the stile and resume your original direction down a long grass field. Once beyond the houses to your left, bear left to a stile at the road. Bear right for the last few yards back to the Three Horseshoes. ■

Hagworthingham & Bag Enderby

This easy ramble explores Hagworthingham and Bag Enderby. It is a good outing for children who will discover fords to cross and a mysterious hollow tree to investigate.

The lovely scenery of this corner of Lincolnshire provided inspiration for the poet Alfred Lord Tennyson, whose father George Tennyson, was rector at nearby Somersby between 1808 and 1831 where Alfred was born in August 1809. The countryside enjoyed during his childhood kept resurfacing in his work many years after he had left Lincolnshire, an example being one of his best known poems "The Brook", published in 1855. Our walk twice crosses the infant River Lymm, considered to be the brook in question, which rises in "haunts of coot and hern" near Somersby to "chatter over stoney ways" and "join the brimming river". Tennyson of course went on to become Poet Laureate in 1850. He died in 1892.

There are Tennyson connections with Bag Enderby too for George was also rector there and in St. Margaret's church a Tennyson display features a large map of the River Lymm. The church itself is quite picturesque, a higgledy-piggledy patchwork of brick and Spilsby Sandstone, known as "greenstone" because it contains the mineral glauconite, which after quarrying and exposure to the air weathers to a khaki green colour. St. Margaret's dates from 1407 and was built with money bequeathed by one Albinus de Enderby. It contains some interesting medieval stained glass, believed to come from Crowland Abbey, and although Albinus had connections

with Crowland no one is entirely sure how or when it was acquired. Another curiosity is part of a Saxon shield fixed to the porch door.

The large, hollow tree stump nearby appears to be the remains of the large tree in an 1889 photograph (shown in Andrew Wheatcroft's book "The Tennyson Album") that was clearly very ancient even then. Village legend is that John Wesley preached beneath the tree and that the Tennyson children (amongst many other generations no doubt!) climbed in its branches.

"Hag" is the local name for Hagworthingham. Back in the village look out for the fine 18th century house of "Hag Newhall" on the corner of Church Lane, and a few yards further on, towards the inn, there is the "Old Hall" with some wonderfully ornate brickwork.

Walk 9

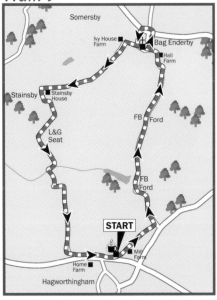

Follow this lane (which becomes a track) all the way to Bag Enderby crossing two fords on the way, each with a footbridge; though, if the water is sufficiently low, children (of any age!) might enjoy the paddle! The second of these fords is through the River Lymm (Tennyson's "Brook"). The track eventually bends left entering Bag Enderby near the church. Explore the village by turning right before the church and take the first left. At the next corner, on a small triangular green, is the ancient hollow tree mentioned above. Now turn left again to visit the church.

To leave Bag Enderby take the "No Through Road" opposite the church and turn left onto a track by a thatched cottage. On reaching a sleeper bridge cross it or the footbridge to its left (this is the Lymm again!) and go left a few paces before turning right up a field edge with a ditch to your right. At the top turn left, then right through the edge of some woods before keeping straight ahead to join a track up to the farmyard of Stainsby House.

ABOUT THE WALK

START : Carpark of the George and Dragon, Hagworthingham. [GR346696]

OS MAPS : Landranger 122 (Skegness) : Explorer 273.

DISTANCE : 4 miles : 6.5 kilometres.

REFESHMENTS : George and Dragon, Hagworthingham

Once in the George & Dragon carpark walk away from the main road onto a track past farm buildings and towards a house. There a footpath begins passing to the right of the garden and going via stiles over two fields to join a lane. Turn left.

Beyond the farm buildings turn left again onto another track. Head downhill for a quarter of a mile to a waymark directing you to the left along a field edge. (This is opposite a lake where a variety of wildfowl can usually be seen and which has a lovely view across the water towards Ashby Puerorum.) At a footbridge and stile cross into the next field, first turning right along the bottom edge, then bearing left steeply uphill. An obvious path continues to a hedge corner below the brow of the hill. Bear right and head over the hilltop into a lane and then down towards Hagworthingham.

At the "old" main road turn left. You will soon join the modern one through the village back to the start. ■

Hagworthingham, Snipe Dales & Winceby

Lincolnshire, for all its history, has witnessed few events of national significance. Amongst them however was the Battle of Winceby on 11th October 1643 during the English Civil War. We visit the battle site.

Although overshadowed by greater battles such as Naseby and Edgehill the Battle of Winceby was nevertheless a crucial victory for Cromwell for its result secured most of eastern England for the Parliamentary cause. The battle took place over a broad sweep of hillside to the west of Snipe Dales. At one point it seemed that history might have turned out quite differently when Cromwell's horse was shot from under him, and Sir Ingram Hopton, a Cavalier commander, stood over Cromwell demanding his surrender. But Hopton was borne away in the mêlée and killed. The Cavalier army was gradually overwhelmed and the battle turned into a rout with a panic stricken retreat towards Horncastle where men and horses were trapped against the high parish boundary hedge between Winceby and Scrafield whose only gate opened towards the fleeing troops and was held shut by the crush. Hundreds were slaughtered in an area still known as "Slash Hollow". Just beyond Winceby garage the road is still named "Slash Lane". Magnanimous in victory however Cromwell ordered a funeral with honours for Hopton at St. Mary's, Horncastle. Nearby the large Victorian edifice of Winceby House has a memorial to the battle on the front lawn. Winceby village itself has all but disappeared but near the entrance to Snipe dales is the abandoned churchyard of St. Margaret's. The latest church on this site, built in 1860 when Winceby still had 78 inhabitants, was demolished in 1964.

In Snipe Dales local Spilsby Sandstone, also known as "Greenstone" overlies Kimmeridge Clay. This produces dry, well-drained slopes with marshy habitats in the low lying parts and a consequent diversity of flora and fauna. There are numerous interpretation boards within the reserve.

Hagworthingham has several buildings of interest, notably the Old Hall with its ornate brickwork nearly opposite the inn, and the New Hall on the corner of Church Lane. Holy Trinity churchyard too is passed towards the end of this walk. With seats and a fine view it provides a welcome resting place before climbing back through the village. The church though retaining some Norman features was restored in 1859 by the famous Louth architect James Fowler, but looks somewhat incomplete since the tower collapsed in 1975.

This walk has another unusual feature in that it crosses from the eastern to the western hemisphere – and back again; look out for the Greenwich Meridian markers in Snipe Dales. (The meridian is shown on the Explorer map.)

NOTE. The walk distance may be halved by starting at Snipe Dales Country Park. Use the path behind the huts at the main carpark, going down to a stream then uphill to join the main walk at approximately GR332686.

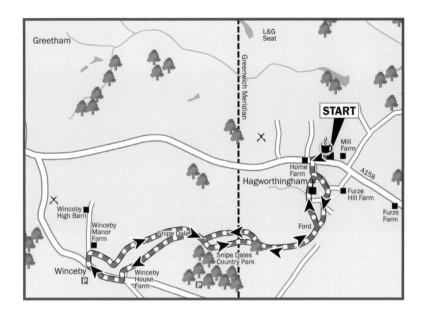

ABOUT THE WALK

START : George and Dragon, Hagworthingham. [GR346696]

OS MAPS : Landranger map 122 (Skegness) : Explorer 273.

DISTANCE : 5 miles : 8 kilometres.

REFRESHMENTS : George and Dragon, Hagworthingham.

From the inn cross the main road and turn right, then left down Church Lane and left again along Bond Hayes Lane. Keep right at the junction and when the road bends go left into The Manor drive. In a few yards climb the stile on the right and beyond a pond descend through meadows to a stream.

Cross the footbridge and turn right, going straight over the road by the ford onto another footpath. This is easily followed by the stream and over grassland to the access point for Snipe Dales Country Park.

Just inside the park turn right. This track soon bears left through the trees along a hilltop. Continue (ignoring colour coded walk routes) for almost half a mile to a path junction where you must turn left or right.

Walk 10

Turn right to descend steps, following a clear path until a public Right of Way is met. (Green and yellow arrow waymarks) Turn left uphill to a stile and cross a large meadow, aiming for the field corner near Winceby House. Turn right along the road for 300 yards, then right again into a lane near the garage.

In 150 yards a signed path on the right (with a special "battle" waymark) goes across another meadow. Aim right of the house seen ahead, crossing two stiles to join a path entering the nature reserve. Turn left, through the abandoned churchyard and descend steeply down into Snipe Dales, following the path and stream until the public footpath waymarks are met again.

Cross the stream to return along your outward route and back up the steps. This time keep ahead, descending to a footbridge. Do not cross it (unless doing the short route) but turn left instead, through a picnic area to a track leading back to your original entry point: then return to Hagworthingham ford.

Finally turn left up the road, past the church into Hagworthingham village and back to the start. ■

Ruckland, The Bluestone Heath Road & Farforth

The origins of the Bluestone Heath Road stretch back into Lincolnshire's prehistoric past. It's an important route over the Wolds and offers superlative views for both drivers and ramblers alike.

The Bluestone Heath Road runs between Burgh-le-Marsh and Ludford, where it linked to another prehistoric track connecting South Ferriby and Horncastle. It traverses some of the Lincolnshire's loftiest countryside and our walk includes a section of this scenic route through stunning countryside. After the walk readers might also like to drive to the magnificent viewpoint situated at GR317762.

We begin this fairly strenuous walk at Ruckland church, situated about 2 miles north of Tetford and right beside the Greenwich Meridian. There is limited parking, so please be considerate when leaving your vehicle. For refreshments the welcoming White Hart Inn in Tetford

is nearest but there are inns at nearby Burwell (The Stag) or Belchford (The Blue Bell).

Ruckland's name translates from the Old Norse language as the "grove of the rooks"; "hrokr" meaning rook and "lundr" a grove. The Scandinavian connection is further emphasised by the dedication of the tiny church here to the Norse saint, St. Olave; the only such one in Lincolnshire. The Son of King Harald, this Norwegian prince joined Viking raiding parties around Europe from the tender age of twelve, and in 1014 AD came to England as a mercenary fighting alongside Ethelred against the Danes. He became king of Norway in 1016 AD reigning for fourteen years until he died, not

entirely unexpectedly, in battle. However in stark contrast to his warlike lifestyle he was renowned for being "diligent in his zeal" in spreading the Christian faith and was made a saint around 1086 AD, over half a century after his death. The church that we see today cost only £400 in 1885, but is in a sense much older for it was largely built from stone salvaged from a former church. Of particular interest is a circular west window and part of a medieval stone coffin set into the north wall. The beautiful oak door was made by local craftsman Peter Davis.

The "by" suffix to Worlaby's name betrays Scandinavian links too of course. Here the little brick church of St. Clement (1873) is now redundant, and only seen distantly across a field near Worlaby House. There is no public access.

Farforth's name comes from the nearby location of a ford, presumably in the valley into which our walk descends upon leaving the Bluestone Heath Road. A village here is mentioned in the Domesday Book but nowadays only Farforth House Farm, plus a lonely house or two and the church remain. It is known that in the late 1700s St. Peter's was in a wretched state and that it continued to deteriorate until by 1847 the roof was leaking badly. It was still another fourteen years however before it was completely rebuilt in 1861, but not very well it would seem, for major structural repairs were again needed by 1904.

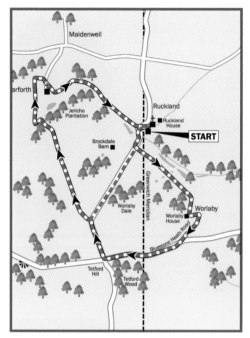

right, going uphill and then round to the left to avoid the farm at Worlaby House. Soon turn right in order to skirt round the far side of the farm buildings. Once beyond these look out for a stile on your right (Worlaby church is easily seen from here). From it cross a long meadow diagonally to the far right hand corner and there join the Bluestone Heath Road.

Turn right, admiring the magnificent views on either side as you proceed, especially over the deep valley to your right. Our route crosses the Greenwich Meridian here and then reaches a crossroads.

Turn right here, initially heading back towards Ruckland. (The road is a short cut.) In 400 yards however, beyond some trees, take the signposted track on the left. In a further mile, as this starts to descend more steeply, look for a waymark on the left, near woods called the Jericho Plantation. The path here drops steeply (and is slippery if wet) to cross the stream at the bottom. Bear

ABOUT THE WALK

START Ruckland church [GR333781]

OS MAPS : Landranger 122 (Skegness) : Explorer 273.

DISTANCE : 5 miles : 8 kilometres.

REFRESHMENTS : None on route.

From St. Olave's at Ruckland set off steeply downhill on the road. When this begins to climb again bear left along a side road for Worlaby. After half a mile, and beyond some lakes, the lane swings

left a few yards to meet a wide footpath linking Oxcombe with Farforth. Turn right along this, climbing beyond Farforth House to a 3-way fingerpost before turning right again above the farm buildings.

At the road go right a few yards and then left down the track beside the churchyard. Follow this into the valley floor until it reaches a stream. Don't cross the stream but veer left (more or less straight ahead really!) with trees close to your right. In half a mile you will be back to Ruckland, opposite St. Olave's where you cross the Greenwich Meridian again. ■

Scamblesby Circuit

Occasionally an opportunity arises to explore previously inaccessible countryside and see familiar views from a new perspective. The opening of several linked permissive routes in the beautiful valley at Scamblesby provides just such an opportunity.

The area around Scamblesby village is of course part of the Wolds Area of Outstanding Natural Beauty, and has been since 1973. The scenery lives up to this reputation too and has the Viking Way threading its way through towards Horncastle, Lincoln and ultimately to County Rutland. The permissive paths used on this walk do not appear on the OS maps and have been created under the DEFRA Countryside Stewardship scheme. There are information maps at access points; access currently lasts until 2014.

Reader's intent on doing this walk should however take stout footwear for some of it may prove rough and muddy in places; but that's a small price to pay for the fabulous views! For those with a picnic the especially good viewpoint at GR276773 (near a pond) overlooks the whole broad amphitheatre of the Scamblesby valley. Note too that a couple of short cuts are mentioned in the route description. We start from the carpark of the Green Man inn by kind permission of the landlord. (He would prefer it if walkers could confirm first by telephone – 01507-343282)

Scamblesby itself is an ancient settlement, proof of this being the "by" suffix to its Scandinavian style name. It might have something of a dark past too, for according to *"A Dictionary of Lincolnshire Place Names"* (K. Cameron), the name may derive from the Old Norse for the homestead of "Skammlaus", meaning the "shameless one". It was

also recorded in the 1086 Domesday Book as "Scamelesbi" so there is a long and rich history. Further proof also appears in the physical evidence of the surrounding landscape with medieval field systems along its outlying slopes.

The first of these features is seen early in the walk by looking eastwards to Rowgate Hill (GR296787) where level terraces, the remains of cultivated medieval fields, can be seen along the hillside. Their date is uncertain, and could be anywhere between the "Conquest" and the early 1500s, but these fields would have been about 12 feet wide at vertical intervals of 8 to 10 feet. There is a similar pattern a little further on at Gaumer Hill (GR289779) though here, where the original terraces were possibly a little narrower and more widely separated, they have unfortunately been damaged by ploughing.

We also see Scamblesby's little church of St. Martins (1893) standing amongst trees on a hilltop to the south of the village. (Also reached by walking up Church Lane) It was rebuilt in 1893 and a plaque on the tower commemorates this. If you are lucky enough to be able to get inside you will see some Norman stonework and old carved bench ends.

And finally! On the natural history front look in the ditches by the path as you climb the hill towards the main viewpoint for a profusion (you can hardly miss them!) of plants known to us as horsetails and which have the Latin botanical name of Equisetum palustre. Although common their interest lies in the fact that they are a very ancient species being virtually identical to plants appearing abundantly in the fossil record from the coal measures, known geologically as the Carboniferous Period, which ended some 350 million years ago.

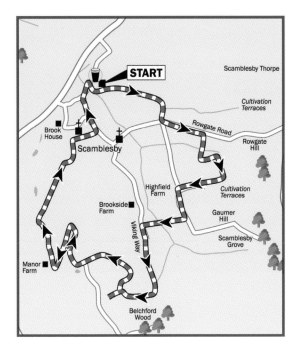

to reach the public road. (Views to the left here include Rowgate Hill.)

Turn left for a quarter of a mile and look for the first permissive path access map on your right just before a cottage; go through the gate. (The next section gives dramatic close-ups of Gaumer Hill.) After the third gate bear left to the field corner, then turn right uphill and join a track. Now turn right below Gaumer Hill, continuing to a track junction and turn left. Just after a white house take the field edge footpath to your right. From a hedge corner walk ahead to soon pass a house and garden to another gate near the end of a surfaced lane. (Following the lane leads back into Scamblesby a mile away.)

To continue the main walk double back left onto a farm track (the Viking Way) and continue to the next access

ABOUT THE WALK

START : Green Man, Scamblesby. [GR278790]

OS. MAP : Landranger 122 (Skegness) : Explorer 273.

DISTANCE : 6 miles : 9.6 kilometres.

REFRESHMENTS : Green Man, Scamblesby.

From the inn carpark turn right and at once go right again on a footpath behind the inn itself. Follow this to a footbridge that leads onto a farm road and there turn right

map. At this point you will need to turn and look behind you. A few feet away is a hedge gap on the left; go to this and return behind the hedge to where the field edge sweeps away in a long arc round to the right, (look for horsetails here) before making some left turns and finally going steeply uphill to meet a public right of way. Cross this, continuing uphill to a copse and pond for the best view of the walk.

Carry on around the hilltop, eventually descending by a hedge and meeting the right of

way again at a 4-way footpath sign. Go through the hedge. (Turning right now gives another easily followed route back into Scamblesby.)

Otherwise turn left going along the opposite side of the hedge to which you have just walked. At the hedge corner keep forward over an arable field into Manor Farm. There turn right onto a grassy track and at two waymarks keep ahead, now with a hedge to your right. Go right at the next waymark along a track until reaching a hedge gap near a paddock. Go through this; then bear left around the paddock where a final right turn brings you past Scamblesby churchyard. Just past the church descend to a lane and turn left back into the village. ■

South Elkington & Acthorpe

Readers get two walks for the price of one here for this route creates a "figure of eight" based on South Elkington, so do them as one long(ish) walk or separately; either "loop" makes an easy walk in grand scenery.

These are both good winter walks too and this is especially true of the first loop, which can be done entirely on virtually traffic free roads and lanes; the second avoids arable land though there may be some mud in Elkington Woods.

Walk "A" around Acthorpe utilizes permissive access to farm roads, granted for the "Round Louth Walk", a 15 mile circular walk created several years ago. We leave the A631 road near the site of an old brickyard at Brickyard Cottages and once on Acthorpe Top, near woods with the delightful name of Fanthorpe Nooking, there are wonderful views towards Louth (with St. James spire prominent) and then far-reaching views to the marsh beyond Fotherby develop too. Acthorpe was a village in medieval times but now only a farm remains. The site is mysterious however because it was not mentioned in the Domesday Book (AD 1086), even though its Danish style place-name seemingly predates the Norman Conquest. Records mention "Achetorp" in the early 14th century so it may previously have been regarded as part of South Elkington. As you return to South Elkington look for the group of three memorial cedar trees (Cedrus Deodora) near the lane, a species recognized by its characteristic drooping top. These young specimens will eventually reach eighty feet in height. Look out too for South Elkington's war memorial, unusually proclaiming that the Great War ended in 1919!

Walk "B" passes All Saints' church, South Elkington, but those doing Walk "A" should give it a visit too. At the imposing lytchgate look to your right to see a Honey Locust tree (Gleditsia) a rarity in this country with huge, vicious thorns up to five inches in length. As a reminder of Christ's crown of thorns it is sometimes known as a "Calvary Tree". Of particular interest inside the church is the glorious chancel ceiling divided into four sections, each sub-divided into four gilded wreaths containing portraits of apostles, angels, prophets and martyrs and painted surrounds to the chancel windows. Behind the tower a small gate is dedicated to a local policeman.

The parkland surrounding Elkington dates from Victorian times when plant hunters were returning to England with many new species and it was the fashion to plant these in landscaped parkland. Trees here include specimens of Coastal Redwoods native to California and Oregon, first available in the 1850s, which can live for thousands of years and grow to over 300 feet in height.

There is only limited parking in where both walks begin – so do park considerately! Refreshments are available at the shop-cum-tearoom and in nearby Louth.

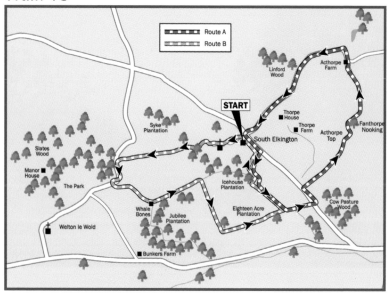

ABOUT THE WALK

START : Church Lane, South Elkington (near the shop). [GR297884]

OS MAPS : Landranger 122 (Skegness) : Explorer 282.

DISTANCE : (Walk A) 3 miles : 4.8 kilometres.

(Walk B) 3 miles : 4.8 kilometres.

REFRESHMENTS : Shop and tearoom at South Elkington.

WALK A Turn right down the main road; preferably crossing over to use the pavement on the far side. In approximately 300 yards re-cross to a signposted track which winds down past the lake in Elkington Park. Beyond it turn left and continue to a footbridge with a stile at either end; cross this and veer slightly right up to another stile by the main road. Cross over and follow the pavement leftwards for a few yards to a farm lane on your right, there is a "Round Louth Walk" permissive waymark on the road sign. (You can also get here along the pavement beside the main road; then turn left!)

Follow the lane uphill passing through a farm to reach Acthorpe

front of the farmhouse. From a stile keep forward in a meadow between grassy knolls and join a track through woods at a fieldgate on your right. When the track goes left keep forward on a grassy headland by a hedge to two metal bridlegates; continue to a third gate and then turn right on a track to the road.

Go left for 300 yards and then left again along a signed track to a junction at a 3-way footpath sign near two whalebones. Now bear left through woodland. At the second footpath sign (near a seat) turn right up an estate road. At the top, where the road bears left there are magnificent views across the Wolds towards Tathwell and to the Bluestone Heath Road. When the road bears right, keep forward on grass to a stile then walk downhill across the park with views ahead to Acthorpe Top on Walk "A". Turn right at the bottom alongside a fence until you can take a footpath going right past the end of the lake. A track now winds up to the road. Go left back to the start. ■

where you should turn left at the public road. In just over a mile this leads back to South Elkington. To conclude your walk stroll along Church Lane to see the church; you will be doing this anyway if you are tackling Walk "B".

WALK B Walk away from the main road. At the church go through the lytchegate bearing right beyond the tower to exit near a pond. Walk round this (in either direction) to a footpath sign near Church Farm and proceed across the

South Ferriby & Horkstow

One aim with our walks is to encourage readers into parts of Lincolnshire that they might not otherwise explore. This walk in the very north of Lincolnshire near South Ferriby partly fits the bill.

Part of the route is along the Viking Way and gives stupendous views over the Ancholme Valley, Read's Island and across the Humber into Yorkshire. The views alone justify the effort and we also see a unique suspension bridge. We start from the carpark situated opposite the pub; picnics are possible on the bank of the New River Ancholme, near Horkstow Bridge or beside the Humber.

One of Horkstow's claims to fame is the suspension bridge over the New River Ancholme. Work to create this straight, navigable waterway began in 1825, though Ferriby Sluice, the final link with the Humber, wasn't finished until 1844. However the meandering course of the "old" river is still traceable even on today's OS maps. The famous civil engineer John Rennie planned the entire scheme, and Horkstow Bridge was his only suspension bridge design. It is therefore of national historic importance and has been restored with new timber decking and in brightly painted red and green ironwork. On completion Ferriby Sluice became the terminus both for Humber ferries and the packet boats, which voyaged inland to Brigg until just before WWI. It is now a marina for pleasure boats.

The walk also passes the walled grounds of Horkstow Hall. During garden landscaping here in the 1790s a magnificent 18 feet long Roman mosaic depicting a chariot race was unearthed and it is now in the British Museum. Any Roman settlement here would have been linked to the Ermine Street that

linked London with York and which used a ferry at Winteringham Haven only four miles away.

High above South Ferriby the path passes Middlegate quarry, which opened in 1938 and now extends to some 150 acres. Successive layers of clay, sand and iron pyrites are quarried, along with the uppermost layers of chalk and all are used in making cement at the large factory seen far below beside the Humber. The Viking Way passes over the conveyor belt that connects them. The bottom of the quarry (unseen) is

now lower than the bed of the Humber.

Further on South Ferriby's church stands on the hillside above the village. Outwardly St. Nicholas's seems all 18th century brick but there is some Norman stonework, including a figure, reputedly of the saint himself. Because of its sloping site the church is aligned north to south rather than the usual east to west; the churchyard can be accessed from the Viking Way. The walk's best views are from the hilltop here overlooking Read's Island.

This, legend says, began to form around 1820 as silt accumulated around a sunken French schooner. The island had grown to 75 acres by 1840 and to 450 acres by 1886 and a solitary farmhouse was eventually built on it named after its first tenant farmer. Remarkably there was a spring for fresh water, but farm animals, people and all supplies relied on ferries for the crossing. Ferriby and Winteringham parishes share the island and it constantly changes its shape through erosion and deposition.

The walk ends along the Humber bank, often in close proximity to shipping for a deepwater channel runs close inshore here. To complete your day out why not visit the newly opened modem Waterside Visitor Centre and nature reserve at nearby Barton?

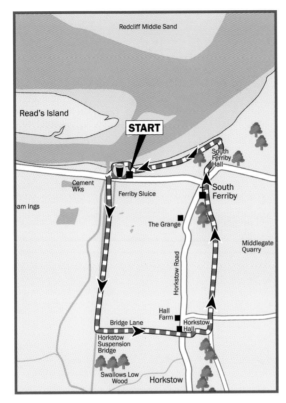

From the carpark entrance turn left and left again down steps to the marina, having the New River Ancholme on your right. Continue through boatyards until a riverside path develops; follow this to John Rennie's suspension bridge. Go up to Bridge Lane and turn left following it for half a mile to its junction with the B1204 road. (On the corner is the walled garden of the Hall.)

Cross the road to a kissing gate and map for a conservation area open to the public. Keep forward up meadows (though there is right to roam) to a gate on your left. Go through this and then continue uphill beside a hedge to a gate and stile at the top. In the lane beyond turn left and at a "T" junction cross onto the track opposite. This is the Viking Way and leads on past Middlegate Quarry before descending

ABOUT THE WALK

START : Countryside Commission carpark, Ferriby Sluice. [GR976210]

OS MAPS : Landranger 112 (Scunthorpe) : Explorer 281.

DISTANCE : 5 miles : 8 kilometres.

REFRESHMENTS : Hope and Anchor, South Ferriby.

to the A1077 at South Ferriby. Now cross into Cliff Road.

This soon becomes become a track and at the first footpath sign turn left down a field edge towards the Humber. From the stile at the bottom turn left again beside the reed beds to another stile near South Ferriby Hall. Climb this to follow the Humber bank for a mile back to Ferriby Sluice. Finally turn left back to the road, the Hope and Anchor and the carpark where we started. ■

South Ormsby, Brinkhill & Driby

At South Ormsby wonderful Wolds scenery provides the setting not only to this picturesque village but those of Brinkhill and the remote settlement of Driby which we also visit.

There is room for considerate roadside parking at the start, and of course the nearby inn makes a convenient place for refreshments before or after your walk. For picnics try above Brinkhill [GR374731], by the ford near Driby [GR380738] or in the wide green lane approaching Driby itself.

The architectural style of the cottages with their matching windows, round-topped and all painted black and white, confirm South Ormsby to be an estate village and it has been the Massingberd family seat since 1638. The present hall, built in 1752, was designed by James Paine and had three floors until the 1920s when the upper one was removed. The school, built in 1858, is now the village hall and is similarly painted black and white, as is the Massingberd Arms.

There is quite a different atmosphere a mile away when we reach Brinkhill. As you enter the village there is a colourful local history information board and then pretty, redbrick cottages and farms occupying a quiet valley mentioned in the Domesday Book. St. Philip's church however is relatively modern, dating from 1857, its simple design boldly emphasized in stripes of brick and sandstone.

When we reach Driby a sense of antiquity is obvious for here is a place where history creates its own mood. The Domesday Book records sufficient cultivated land for twelve ploughs, with sixty acres of meadow, a mill and a population approaching a hundred. Many more than now! The village once straddled the green lane along which we make our approach and the

manor house, though dating from the 17th century, occupies a medieval moated site. Here St. Michael's church is Victorian too (1849), but redundant since 1974 and now converted into a striking private house with additional wings and towers.

Back in South Ormsby St. Leonard's church on its hilltop is certainly worth a visit. Of special interest is a south aisle window of French (or possibly Flemish) 16th century glass with its own special interpretive display. Local tradition is that it was obtained from Notre Dame in Paris during the French Revolution. Parishioners' craftwork on display takes the form of colourful kneelers depicting biblical symbols, village houses and wildlife. South Ormsby can also lay claim to Samuel Wesley as its rector before he moved to Epworth, where his famous sons John and Charles were born. Many grander churches would envy such a wealth of history.

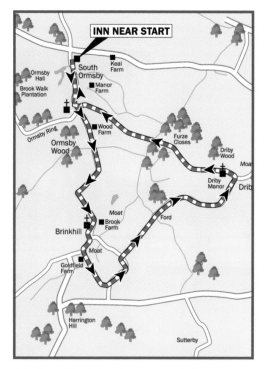

INN NEAR START

Ormsby Hall
Brook Walk Plantation
South Ormsby
Keal Farm
Manor Farm
Wood Farm
Ormsby Ring
Ormsby Wood
Furze Closes
Driby Wood
Moat
Driby Manor
Drib
Moat
Brook Farm
Ford
Brinkhill
Moat
Goldfield Farm
Harrington Hill
Sutterby

ABOUT THE WALK

START : Park near the Massingberd Arms, South Ormsby.

OS MAPS : Landranger 122 (Skegness) : Explorer 273.

DISTANCE : 5 miles : 8 kilometres.

REFRESHMENTS : Massingberd Arms, South Ormsby.

Facing the Massingberd Arms turn right to walk through South Ormsby to the old school. (On the right here is a footpath to the church. As we return to this point you could visit it later.) A few yards further on is a road junction; bear left here for a mile of quiet, easy walking to Brinkhill.

Keep right at the junction just after Brinkhill church and in 200 yards look for a footpath sign and stile on the left before Goldfield Farm. A narrow path passes behind farm buildings to emerge in a paddock. Walk up its left hand edge to another stile and then directly across a small arable field before continuing steeply uphill through woodland, first on a boardwalk and then steps. (Look back here for marvellous views.)

Continue until a fingerpost points left towards a lane a few yards away with more fine views as you walk a short way downhill before turning right onto a signposted track. Follow this for about a mile, with a ford and footbridge about half way along, until another path joins from the

hillside on the right. Now bear left down to Driby's huge open green and turn left again over a cattle grid.

Beyond the church a track leads to a Water Board pumping station entrance. Ignore the footpath bearing left and climb the stile in front of you, keeping forward by a fence. Where this ends veer slightly right over an arable field (the way is usually marked in any crops) aiming for a protruding corner of Furze Closes wood. Within the woods a narrow path soon becomes a track. At the far side a grassy track continues forward for 250 yards into a large meadow with a farm seen ahead.

Now bear half right towards a stile in a fence by two large trees. Cross another meadow to a gate and from it aim slightly left over the third field towards the far top corner. There you will find another stile and a path through the rear of a cottage garden; beyond that bear left down a paddock, emerging opposite South Ormsby church. Turn right back to the start. ■

Spilsby & Halton Holegate

This walk is on the very fringes of the Wolds, starting on high ground in Spilsby itself and descending to the fen edge to a quiet corner of Lincolnshire that remains relatively unexplored on foot, but provides easy walking nevertheless.

We begin from the public carpark in Post Office Lane, Spilsby which is itself off Queen Street at the east end of the Market Place. There is a charming pub a third of the way round at Halton Holegate and plenty of cafés and pubs when you return to Spilsby.

Halton Holegate's name, from the Old English, refers to its "hollow way", the road that still descends between rocky cliffs to the fens. The present St. Andrew's church, built around A.D. 1400, has an imposing tower of local, "green" sandstone. Relics inside, many older than the church, include a 14th century font, an ancient alms box hewn from a single oak beam and monuments to an "Unknown Warrior" and to Sir Walter Bec whose family were

landowners here from the 12th century. The churchyard gives extensive views over the fens.

Along Peasgate Lane [GR 410646] we cross the abandoned line of the Firsby and Spilsby Railway. (The nearby house is obviously railway architecture.) This 4 mile long branch line opened in 1868 with passenger services surviving until 1939 and goods until 1958. Once back in town part of Spilsby's station is still visible in the industrial estate on your right, just before you reach the church.

Spilsby is unique in Lincolnshire by having three market places. In the "West" Market stands the White Hart, an old mall and coaching inn with its l8th century mailbox still built into the front wall, and the 1861 Franklin

memorial. In the "Central" Market, only 150 years ago, you could buy or sell a wife along with your market produce – ten shillings being a typical price. And the "East" Market still has its 14th century cross.

Sir John Franklin, born on 16th April 1786, is Spilsby's most famous son. He joined the navy aged fourteen and within his first five years service had spent three exploring Australia with Matthew Flinders, and been with Nelson at both Copenhagen and Trafalgar. His fame however rests upon his exploits as he attempted to find the Northwest Passage round Canada, beginning with a voyage in 1818 and continuing with others in 1819 and 1825. His final trip was in 1845, when aged nearly fifty. After two bitter winters trapped in pack ice he died and his crew, having abandoned ship, perished after being reduced to eating their leather boots. Relics discovered record Franklin's death on 11th June 1847, but his body has never been located. Modem atlases still show natural features in northern Canada bearing his name. A plaque on the wall of the bakery (opposite the Central Market) marks his birthplace and bright coloured panels on the wall of the public toilets opposite supply more information about him.

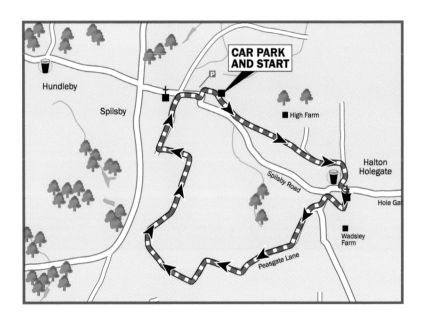

ABOUT THE WALK

START : Carpark in Post Office Lane, Spilsby. [GR405661]

OS MAPS : 122 (Skegness) : Explorer 274.

DISTANCE : 4 miles : 6.5 kilometres.

REFRESHMENTS : The Bell, Halton Holegate.

Numerous cafés and inns in Spilsby.

 Leave the carpark by the footpath at the rear. This passes behind several gardens to reach a small arable field where you should bear half fight to a stile and signpost leading to a short footpath to the B1195 (Wainfleet) road.

Do not join the road but turn left onto a track. (There are fine views along this next section with Boston Stump being visible on a clear day.) Keep directly forward as the track becomes a grassy path and proceed for half a mile along field edges and a second track to reach a metal gate in a hollow. Walk up the hedged lane

beyond to another lane and turn right into Halton Holgate. At a right hand bend either continue for a few yards to "The Bell", or, look for steps ahead down to the "Hollow gate". Cross into the churchyard.

Walk through to the stile at the far side, and disregarding the waymark, turn sharp right towards the field corner where another path leads to the road. Turn left and then in a few yards enter Peasgate Lane on the right, following this for three quarters of a mile (the latter part is unsurfaced) to a track junction. Go left and soon, at another track junction, turn right. (Use the track, not the field path which also branches off here!) After passing a pond cross the footbridge on your right into a meadow. Walk uphill to a

fence, turning left to follow it to a corner and turn right to another stile. Continue by a hedge, then cross a farm track, keeping forward to the edge of Spilsby and a four-way signpost.

Bear left here. On reaching a road turn right to pass the church, and go right again into the West Market. Cross to Franklin's statue. Staying on that side will take you past the plaque at his birthplace as you return to the start. ■

G. BACON. SC
LONDON 1861

Tealby & Walesby

Here we visit the Wolds in order to walk from Tealby, one of Lincolnshire's prettiest villages, and visit Walesby's two historic churches. The scenery is dramatic as we return along the Viking Way – but is quite hilly!

When the Domesday Book was written the streams at "Tavelsbi" were powering fourteen watermills and even today the road towards Binbrook is called Papermill Lane. Parkland to the south of the village once surrounded Bayons Manor, the Gothic mansion of Charles Tennyson D'Eyncourt and uncle to the poet Alfred Tennyson. Built in the 1830s Bayons Manor became derelict after WWII and sadly the remains were dynamited in 1965. However local reminders of the Tennyson family still exist. Tealby's school, of 1856, was paid for, and probably designed by Charles, and family monuments adorn the church. Parts of All Saints' tower are Norman, whilst inside are examples of Early English, Decorated and Perpendicular architectural styles. The pulpit is made from wood retrieved from Bayons Manor.

Walesby is a classic example of a migrating village that was once situated high on the hillside around its church, All Saints, and former village earthworks are still visible. A Roman settlement is also known nearby for a villa has been excavated nearby in 1859 and a Roman lead font was ploughed up in 1959.

However Walesby's need for a "new" church was starkly apparent by the 1880s and a tragic story lies behind the building of St. Mary's down in the "new" village. The rector, the Rev. Percival Laurence, worked tirelessly for 30 years to raise the necessary funds, but at the culmination of his efforts died on the very day that building work began. The interior is most unusual with massive central pillars rising to the

roof ridge; a design that can cause difficulties at weddings and funerals as the churchwardens will testify.

Up on its hilltop site All Saints fell into disuse as the villagers moved away, and was almost demolished in the 1930s, but thankfully was rescued by Canon Harding from Lincoln and still stands, proud but isolated. The atmosphere inside is truly medieval and, because of an unusual window depicting Christ with ramblers and cyclists, is known as the Ramblers church with a religious service taking place here for walkers (and indeed all countryside lovers!) each Trinity Sunday. The Viking Way passes through the churchyard.

The area around the Ramblers church at Walesby has fine views and some adjacent fields have public access agreements; anywhere there makes a good place for a picnic.

NOTE: This route connects with Walk 19 from Walesby to give a full day's walking.

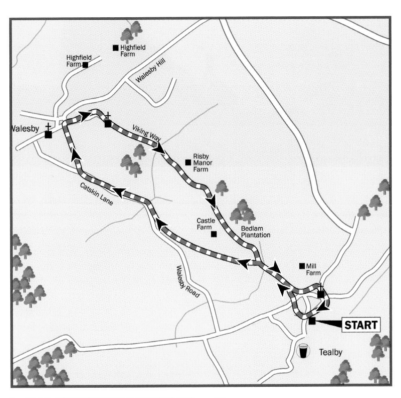

ABOUT THE WALK

START : Tealby village. [Around GR157907]

OS MAPS : Landranger 113 (Grimsby) : Explorer 282.

DISTANCE : 4 miles : 6.5 kilometres.

REFRESHMENTS : Kings Head inn and the tearooms in Tealby.

Park considerately and begin the walk by following the narrow lane that you will find to the left of the butchers shop in Front Street, Tealby. On reaching the main road cross to a footpath, just to your left. Veer left down the first field and in the second field look for a 3-way footpath sign over to your left.

Cross the nearby footbridge and a narrow field to a stile in the far hedge. Follow the marked path over the shoulder of the hill and cross a farm track, continuing by a wire fence. At the field corner go left to a stile, climb over and walk ahead over pasture, crossing another farm road to reach a stile in the far left hand hedge corner. Turn right on the road beyond.

In a quarter of a mile, just before a house, take the footpath on the right, bearing left behind the house. From a stile follow waymarks around a garden to emerge in Walesby. Turn left to visit St. Mary's, Walesby's "new" church 200 yards away, then return.

From the nearby bend a lane climbs to All Saints church. Don't miss looking inside this remarkable building and then continue from the churchyard by going left uphill to a stile, and crossing the next field to another stile. In a few yards descend very steeply before climbing (equally steeply) up the far hillside to pass below Risby Manor. After crossing the farm road keep on high ground as much as possible to enter some woods at a stile.

Exit near Castle Farm (early 19th century and never really a castle) and turn left downhill where you will soon rejoin your outward route. Follow this back into Tealby, but at the road turn left. Go through the churchyard, cross the main road onto Beck Hill where you will find Front Street now to your right. Before returning to your car however it's worth continuing down to the pretty ford at the bottom of Beck Hill. ■

Tetford & Salmonby

This walk from the pretty Wolds village of Tetford could almost be termed a "Lake District" walk as it passes four stretches of water en route and there are fine views westwards to the hills around Fulletby

Begin near Tetford church where roadside parking is possible with the ancient White Hart inn nearby. The route is for a short way on a permissive path not depicted on OS maps. After wet weather parts can be muddy!

Some 10,000 years ago glaciers covered this countryside but following their retreat, prehistoric man moved into these hills. The ancient Bluestone Heath Road is a mile to the north and there was possibly a Neolithic settlement on the nearby flat-topped Hoe Hill. The summit, formed of hard erosion resistant carstone, holds no direct evidence of a hilltop settlement but the surrounding area has yielded many worked flint tools. Arthur Mee in his King's England for "Lincolnshire" mentions a prehistoric site on nearby Nab Hill. Both are clearly visible from Salmonby on the western skyline. Later the Romans built a road from Lincoln to the Wash linking with the Peddars Way in Norfolk.

Tetford's North Street lies on the course of this road, which passed the present day churchyard where, running at right angles to it is the Greenwich Meridian line. Tetford was recorded as "Tesforde" in the Domesday Book and as having a mill, which may have been on the site of the present 17th century watermill seen on the walk. Parts of the White Horse are said to date from the 16th century and it was once the meeting place of the "Tetford Club" for local gentry, including Alfred Tennyson from nearby Somersby. In 1764 they entertained the famous Dr. Johnson.

St. Mary's church, built of local "greenstone", is 14th century with a 15th century tower. The tower clock reputedly came from Winchester School but this is not confirmed in the informative guide. Inside are memorials to members of a branch of the Dymoke family, the king's champions from Scrivelsby, and some 17th century armour. There is another curiosity, outside and to the northeast of the chancel, in the form of a headstone to two gypsies, Tyso Boswell and Edward Hearin, killed by lightning in 1830.

Many prehistoric implements, axe heads and pottery have been found around Salmonby village, but particularly to the northwest and west; roughly where our walk goes after leaving the lake. The medieval settlement of Salmonby stretched down the valley from the southern side of the lake. Salmonby's church once perched above the village but was demolished in 1977; the churchyard however can still be reached by steep steps up a rocky bluff. The organ and altar are preserved in St. Mary's, Tetford. In the barn wall opposite is a (now quite rare) Victorian letterbox.

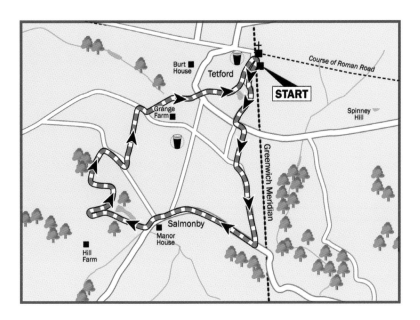

ABOUT THE WALK

START : Near the church, Tetford.
[GR334748]

OS MAPS : Landranger 122
(Skegness) : Explorer 273

DISTANCE : 4 miles : 6.5
kilometres.

REFRESMENTS : White Hart,
Tetford.

From Tetford church walk
down East Road past the inn.
On reaching the junction with South
Road bear left for a few yards to a
stile and footpath signpost on the
right. Follow this path to join a
bridleway, then go left following that
to a road. Turn right here and at a
junction bear left into Salmonby.
Look for the old postbox on the left
and churchyard steps on the right.

Opposite these bear left, shortly
going right at a footpath sign by a
stream. Go along the track to a stile on
the right. Climb over and from a
second stile keep forward passing a
lake, then veering left to a footbridge
over the feeder stream. Climb the far

bank to reach a stile in the fence by large tree.

The "permissive" path begins here. Double back on the far side of this fence and in the field corner by the lake veer left to join a track. At a junction cross to the stile seen in the fence opposite. Keep left along the inside of this fence/hedge (parallel to the track) to the field corner before turning right, past woods and continue downhill to a footbridge at the far end of the field. Walk to the road a few yards away.

Turn right for 300 yards then left from a signpost along a headland path with a hedge to your right. At the next road turn right for 100 yards before going left through a kissing gate. After passing between two lakes (there are picnic tables here) the path bears left slightly before turning sharp right by trees. Follow it to the road in Tetford.

Turn right and almost at once left into Mill Lane. At the end keep forward past the old mill and go left again when a footbridge is reached. Ignoring a path to the left continue by another lake to rejoin East Road and turn left back to the start. ■

Walesby & Normanby-le-Wold

This walk makes a day out in an especially scenic area of the Wolds to visit Normanby-le-Wold, which ranks as Lincolnshire's highest village with the county's highest point (560 feet) being only half a mile further north.

Our route to this tiny village crosses dramatic countryside some of which is within public access areas; the return follows the Viking Way. There are magnificent views throughout and a further plus for many readers will be the scenic Wolds drive to reach Walesby in the first place.

The walk has a lengthy, though gradual, climb to Normanby. (But the views are worth it!) Limited parking is available at Walesby village hall in Otby Lane, but (especially at weekends) try parking near the church where the road is wide enough to permit this, but wherever you park please be considerate to villagers! The tearoom is just down the road from the "new" church and there is another (Wolds View) at the top of Bully Hill by the crossroads above Tealby. Local access areas near

Normanby and the Ramblers church allow freedom to roam so picnics are no problem.

"Walesbi" is an ancient settlement for evidence of a Roman villa has been found on the hill by the "old" church of All Saints and earthworks in the vicinity also betray the location of the medieval village; for over the centuries Walesby has migrated downhill. Thus abandoned, All Saints had the good fortune to escape alteration and retains a genuine medieval atmosphere. In spite of centuries of neglect it was eventually given a complete and sympathetic restoration in the 1930s and since 1932 an annual ramblers Trinity Sunday service has been held there, an event recalled by the unique stained glass window depicting Christ greeting to walkers and cyclists.

Down in the "modern" village a "new" church (St. Mary's) was built in 1913, after many years of campaigning and fund raising by the rector Rev. Laurence who tragically died the very same day that building work began. Large pillars along the central aisle can be an obstacle at weddings and funerals.

The water mill below Otby dates from the C18th and was working until 1945 and traces of the mill leat, which channeled water to an overshot waterwheel, can still be seen.

In 1868 St. Peter's at Normanby-le-Wold was restored externally by the Louth architect James Fowler but inside lots of medieval stonework remains. This includes one pillar bearing a rare (perhaps unique) horn shaped carving, the significance of which has never been convincingly explained. An arch over the south aisle also has a carving of a man apparently in pain with toothache! Across the lane is a small red brick chapel, once the Sunday School, and probably Georgian in age.

Note to that this walk links with Walk 17 from Tealby to provide a longer route.

Walk 19

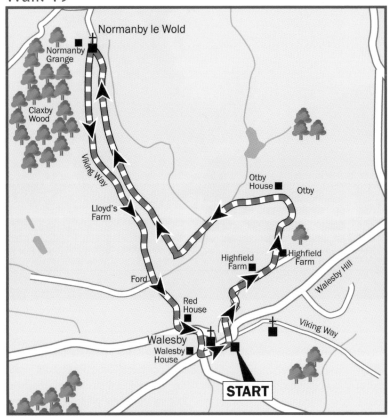

Normanby le Wold

Normanby Grange

Claxby Wood

Viking Way

Lloyd's Farm

Otby House

Otby

Highfield Farm

Highfield Farm

Walesby Hill

Ford

Red House

Walesby

Walesby House

Viking Way

START

ABOUT THE WALK

START : Walesby village. [GR134923]

OS MAPS : Landranger 113 (Grimsby) : Explorer 282.

DISTANCE : 4 miles : 6.5 kilometres.

REFRESHMENTS : Treasure tearooms, Walesby.

Leave Walesby along Otby Lane, passing the entrance to Highfield Farm and continuing until you reach a gate on the left just before Otby House. From it walk downhill, keeping towards the right hand edge of the field. At the bottom use the left hand gate. Keep right to cross a stile and head towards the buildings of Otby Mill, going to the

right of them to a footpath junction just above a footbridge over a stream.

Do not cross the bridge, but instead turn right uphill with a hedge on your left. In a little under half a mile the right of way goes left through a bridlegate in the hedge but a sign shows a permissive footpath ahead; this leads from here to Normanby. (Go through the bridlegate for a short cut back to Walesby; on the other side look uphill for a three-way footpath sign and follow the instructions from (*) below.)

The main walk however continues uphill and along the ridge top, though occasionally dropping to the right slightly for stiles, but always with a hedge or wall not far away on your left. When nearing Normanby-le-Wold church aim slightly leftwards where you will find a stile leading onto a lane. Turn right for the church.

The return route comes back along the lane, passing the stile you climbed earlier to reach another at the lane end. All you need do now is follow the special Viking Way "helmet" waymarks by bearing left along the hilltop. After about three-quarters of a mile the path descends to a stile by a three-way signpost and meets the short route.

(*) From this signpost veer slightly right across a shallow valley and over the shoulder of the slope forming the far side with its exposed rock strata.

Below the hill is another footpath sign and from it bear half left on a track. Continue to the public road. Turn left towards Walesby village.

In a few yards a signed path on the right cuts through to the tearooms with St. Mary's "new" church just to your left. To regain Otby Lane pass the church and take the first turn on the left. Conclude your walk by visiting All Saints (the Ramblers church), found by climbing the lane from the top of the village. ■

Wold Newton & Beesby

In many places the fringes of the Wolds give wonderful views across the marsh to the sea and the hillsides to the east of Wold Newton provide some of the best of these.

Where our walk begins there is only limited roadside parking space so please consider others, including local farmers and the villagers. For refreshments try pubs at Brackenborough, the surrounding villages or Louth, which are all within easy reach.

Lincolnshire holds the distinction of being in the forefront of the investigations and understanding of "Deserted Medieval Villages" – DMV's to archaeologists! Since serious study began over 220 such sites have been identified in the county. Although the existence of "lost" villages had been known for centuries no one realized how many there were until the advent of aerial photography. (The first aerial photograph ever taken of a deserted village was at Gainsthorpe in northwest Lincolnshire on 3rd April

1925.) Initially their disappearance was attributed to the Black Death in 1349 – 1350 but recent opinion is that whilst this was indeed a major factor there were other reasons too, and that, more importantly, their impact varied from place to place. For instance, the rise in sheep farming led to much arable land becoming pasture, and then of course fewer farm workers were needed. There were other economic factors too, such as the improvement of farming techniques and in some cases villages were simply "removed" as wealthy landowners created parklands around their country estates.

The eastern slopes of the Wolds are particularly rich in DMV's. Readers who have the OS Explorer map should easily find six identified sites between Louth and Beesby; and

there were others at such places as Acthorpe and Hawerby. Incidentally further views of Beesby lost village are obtained by continuing along the road a short way from GR269968 before taking the footpath towards "The Valley". (See route instructions.) The outlines of the medieval strip fields are clearly seen from the walk however, especially around GR261963.

Wold Newton itself is situated in a secluded valley and has several old houses built of local chalk. Its little church, All Hallows, is perched high on the hillside and can only be reached by footpaths. There has been a church here since the times of the Danish invasions but the present one was designed by the Louth architect James Fowler and built in 1862. In the porch a rather unusual notice records the receipt of a grant for £50 in 1861 from the Incorporated Society for Buildings and Churches, but stipulations were made, including the number of seats to be provided within, and that they were to be free!

Beesby Woods and the woods through "The Valley" are carpeted with wild garlic, a sure sign of ancient undisturbed woodland and there are squirrels about too! The descent to Beesby provides fine views out over the marsh and as far as the Humber and Spurn Point in clear weather, whilst the return to Wold Newton gives views inland over the Wolds.

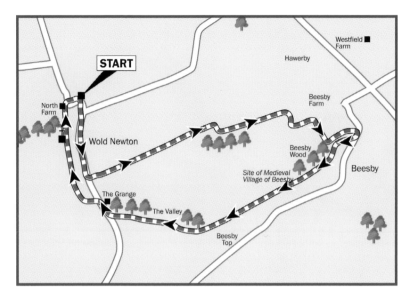

ABOUT THE WALK

START: North end of Wold Newton village. [GR243971]

OS MAPS : Landranger 113 (Grimsby) : Explorer 282.

DISTANCE : 4 miles : 6.5 kilometres.

REFRESHMENTS : None on route.

Walk back through Wold Newton passing a "T" junction until you reach a footpath on the left just after the last cottage (The Waggoners). Follow this uphill to a waymark and continue to the right of the hedge. At a footpath junction go right, then left initially alongside woods. Keep forward downhill with far

reaching views out over the marsh and the Humber to another path junction and there turn right.

Immediately after a copse turn left down a track and right at the first junction. This brings you to Beesby Woods. Turn left and walk down to a road. Turn right for 100 yards to a footpath sign pointing off to the right. (If you wish you may continue along the road a short way for views of part of Beesby DMV. Return to this point.)

Take the signed footpath into an enclosed valley to follow a clear path beside a fence. Go through two gates

at a farmyard and keep forward, still by the fence. There are now more good views to your left of the deserted village earthworks and a little later of its ridge and furrow fields. Keep straight ahead now through two sets of double gates and along a field edge to enter "The Valley" where a good path (that may be muddy after rain) leads to a road.

Turn right and in 200 yards bear left into South Farm, going right to locate a track leaving the back corner of the farmyard. Now keep ahead until you reach the church. Pass in front of the lytchgate maintaining your direction through woods to another farmyard. Go through this to a road and there turn right back to the start. ■